## Pete Jenkins

Guided Reading Level: **S**

## Rourke
### Educational Media

rourkeeducationalmedia.com

Scan for Related Titles and
Teacher Resources

*coconut crab—the largest land-living arthropod in the world*

# TABLE OF CONTENTS

Ever heard of a blobfish? Well, it is one gross-looking creature! Looking like something out of a horror movie, the blobfish belongs to a **species** of fish known as fatheads.

Guess you could say ugly runs in the family!

A BIG BLOB

Just a mass of pale, jelly-like flesh with puffy, loose skin, a big nose and beady eyes, the blobfish looks like a pile of pink mush, unlike any other creature, in or out of the ocean.

Blobfish live in depths up to 3,900 feet (1,189 meters). The normal pressure there is up to 118 times higher than at sea level. They can be found off the coasts of Australia, Tasmania, and New Zealand.

No one has ever seen a blobfish eat. Scientists believe that it feeds on crabs, sea urchins, and shellfish. Since it has no muscles, the blobfish cannot hunt, so it just opens its mouth and sucks in whatever drifts by.

It's not only gross, but pretty lazy too!

# DUMBO THE

The Dumbo octopus is named after Walt Disney's famous character, Dumbo the elephant, because of the ear-like fins that protrude from the sides of its head. Not the most attractive attribute.

Most species of Dumbo octopi are small, usually about eight inches (20.3 centimeters) in length. The largest recorded specimen measured six feet (183 centimeters) in length and weighed 13 pounds (5.90 kilograms). That's a whole lot of ugly!

# OCTOPUS?

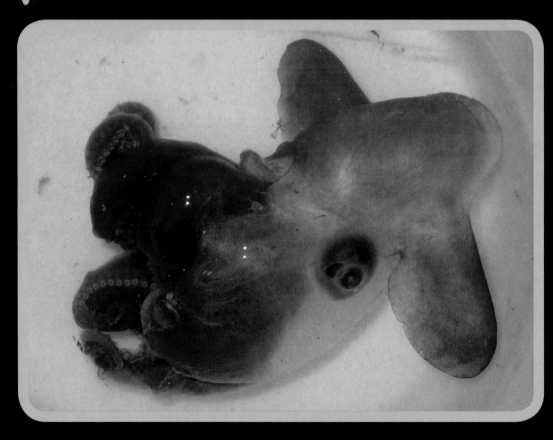

With more than 37 known species, they can be found in almost every ocean around the world. Since not much is known about these octopi, they are considered to be endangered.

The hagfish, sometimes referred to as the slime eel, is not an eel at all. We're not sure whether the hagfish is even a fish! What is known is that the hagfish is one of the most disgusting creatures in the sea.

# SLIME EEL?

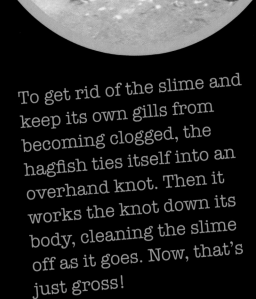

Hagfish have no real predators because of their interesting secret weapon. If a hagfish is threatened, it can excrete large amounts of gelatin-like slime into the water. This slime clogs the gills of fish, suffocating them.

To get rid of the slime and keep its own gills from becoming clogged, the hagfish ties itself into an overhand knot. Then it works the knot down its body, cleaning the slime off as it goes. Now, that's just gross!

UGLY ON

The star-nosed mole has a red-colored ring of fleshy, retractable tentacles surrounding its nose. Its scaly, fleshy tail is covered with rings and short, coarse hairs.

This species hunts and captures their victims so fast, it is almost impossible for humans to follow the action. The tentacles of these species are six times faster than the human hand.

# THE GROUND
## AND ALL AROUND

Originally from the Northeastern parts of the U.S. and Eastern Canada, star-nosed moles are also found in Minnesota, Labrador, and Quebec. They also inhabit regions of the Appalachian Mountains and the Atlantic Coast extending to Southeastern Georgia.

During the winter, its tail swells larger and serves as a fat storage organ.

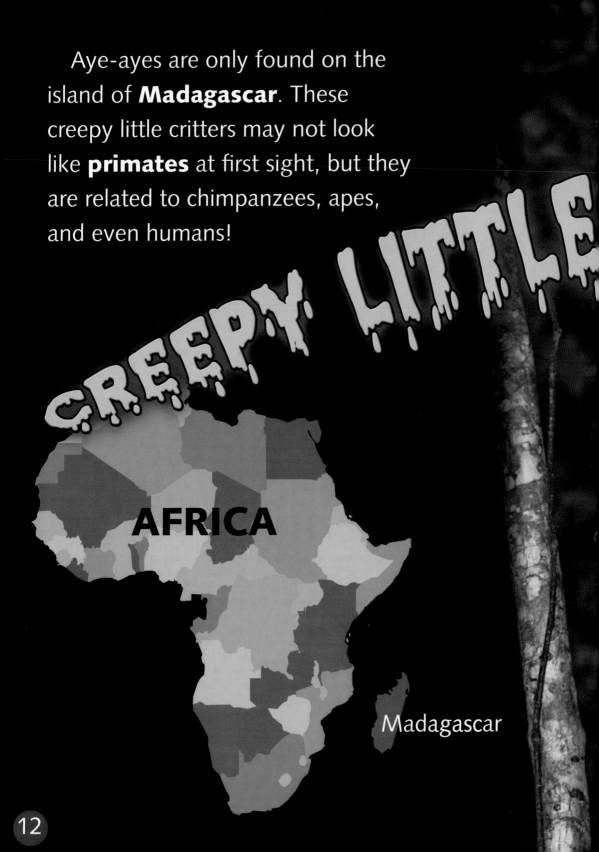

Aye-ayes are only found on the island of **Madagascar**. These creepy little critters may not look like **primates** at first sight, but they are related to chimpanzees, apes, and even humans!

CREEPY LITTLE

AFRICA

Madagascar

CRITTERS

With dark fur, bulging, glow-in-the-dark eyes, and claws that resemble the overgrown nails of a witch, the aye-aye is considered one of the world's ugliest creatures. Some even find it terrifying!

Legend has it aye-ayes wander around human villages at night, sneaking into houses and puncturing the arteries of villagers by using their claws. Seeing one is considered a bad omen, so they are killed on sight. **Yikes!**

FRILLED AND

# FRIGHTENING

Frilled lizards, or frillnecks, are members of the dragon family. They are found in the temperate forests and savannas of Australia. Though these small creatures are less than three feet (91.5 centimeters) in length, they can scare up a big fright!

Its startling brightly colored frill is nearly a foot (30.48 centimeters) across. With its mouth wide open, displaying strong teeth, the frilled lizard looks prehistoric!

Rearing up on its hind legs, it thrashes its tail on the ground, and jumps toward an attacker, hoping to scare it off.

The lizard also has a comical side. If these scare tactics don't work, the lizard simply turns tail, mouth and frill open, and bolts! It continues running without stopping or looking back until it reaches safety.

Female frillnecks lay between eight and 23 eggs in an underground nest. The hatchlings emerge fully independent and capable of hunting and utilizing their frill.

MIND YOUR

Everyone has to deal with flies while eating outside. Although you may not think these pesky, flying distractions are gross, they are disgusting without a doubt! Flies eat **feces**, or poop, and their bodies are covered in bacteria.

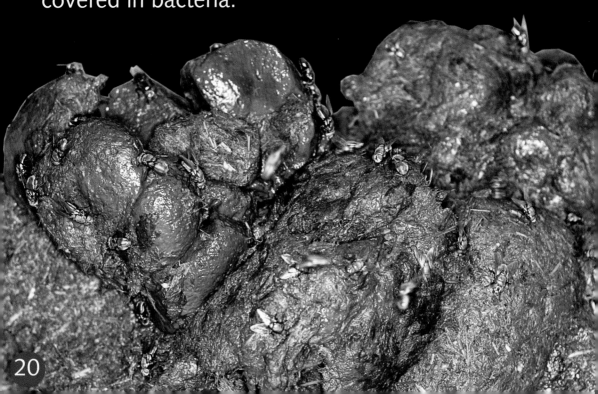

# MANNERS!

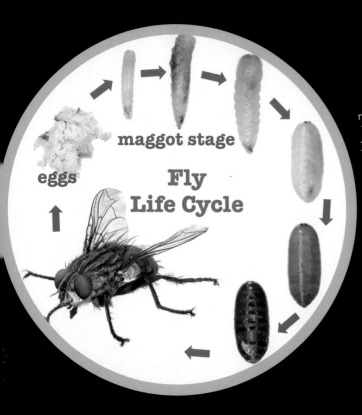

maggot stage

eggs

**Fly
Life Cycle**

The common house fly poops on just about everything it touches. Yuck! Flies also lay their eggs in dead flesh, which hatch to become **maggots**. Hungry yet?

Flies don't just buzz around our food. They vomit on it, puking up enzymes and digestive juices to help break it down into a soupy juice they suck through their straw-shaped tongue. They leave some of their fly puke soup behind for us to share. Thanks very much!

WE WANT TO

# SUCK YOUR BLOOD!

Vampire **bats** are remarkably disease-free animals. Your risk of catching **rabies** or anything else from their bite is unlikely. Just the name may be enough to scare you, though. But wait until you learn what they do.

Vampire bats will feed on the same victim night after night. Scientists have discovered that vampire bats can recognize an individual human by the sound they make when they are breathing. To make things worse, their teeth are so sharp, you won't even feel the bite!

SLITHERING

The brown tree snake is an invasive species introduced to the island of Guam sometime during World War II. It has caused some horrifying problems ever since.

# BABY KILLER

The snakes are so abundant that power lines have been brought down under the weight of the reptiles lying on them.

If that's not terrifying enough, the brown tree snake has become infamous among locals for its habit of attacking children and babies while they sleep.

Scientists are baffled by this behavior. Sleeping children pose no threat to the snakes, and even the smallest, most delicious-smelling baby is too large for a brown tree snake to consume.

**Experiments** have also shown that the snakes are attracted to the smell of blood and will actively seek it out. Doesn't make you feel very safe, does it?

People around the world have to deal with different types of animals every day. Most aren't harmful, but some have pretty gruesome habits! All I can say is,

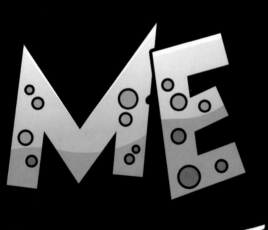

**GROSS**

**ME OUT!**

Sea cucumbers use an interesting technique when they are faced with danger. They expel their internal organs along with a toxic substance called holothurin toward an attacker. Their missing organs grow back in one to five weeks.

**Yuck!**

# GLOSSARY

**bats** (bats): small, flying mammals with leathery wings that
feed at night

**experiments** (ik-SPER-uh-ments): tests to try out a theory
or to see the effect of something

**feces** (FEE-sees): waste that is released from the body of an
animal or human

**Madagascar** (MAD-uh-gahs-car): an island nation off the
southeast coast of Africa

**maggots** (MAG-uhts): larvae of certain flies that look
like worms

**primates** (PRYE-mates): members of the group of mammals
which include monkeys, apes, and humans

**rabies** (RAY-beez): a sometimes fatal disease that can affect
humans, dogs, bats, and other warm-blooded mammals

**species** (SPEE-seez): one of the groups which animals and
plants of the same genus are divided into

# INDEX

# SHOW WHAT YOU KNOW

1. Why do you think the brown tree snake only targets children?
2. What is the aye-aye omen?
3. At what depths of the ocean can the blobfish be found?
4. How did the Dumbo octopus get its name?
5. Name something a vampire bat does. Why do you think they do this?

# WEBSITES TO VISIT

http://kids.nationalgeographic.com/explore/13-facts-to-gross-out-your-parents
www.sciencekids.co.nz/sciencefacts/animals.html
www.planetozkids.com/oban/animals/weird.htm

# ABOUT THE AUTHOR

Pete Jenkins loves your average domesticated pet, but after writing this book he hopes that he NEVER encounters one of these animals. Still cringing at the thought of seeing one makes him grossed out. Before writing this book, he never knew animals could be so CREEPY!

**Meet The Author!**
www.meetREMauthors.com

www.rourkeeducationalmedia.com

PHOTO CREDITS: Cover: Frilled lizard © Matt Cornish-Shutterstock.com, hagfish courtesy of NOAA Okeanos, star-nosed mole © photosmash- i-stockphoto.com, bugs in background on cover and title page © ElliLina-Shutterstock.com; Page 2 © Kristina Vackova -Shutterstock.com; Page 4 Blobfish © NORFANZ Founding Parties and CSIRO Australian National Fish Collection; Page 6 Dumbo octopus Image courtesy of the NOAA's Office of Ocean Exploration and Research., page 7 Dumbo octopus © Mike Vecchione, NOAA; page 8 courtesy of NOAA Okeanos Explorer Program, page 9 courtesy NOAA/CBNMS; page 10 © iStock_Mary Gascho; page 12 map © Vertes Edmond Mihai-Shutterstock.com, pages 13, 14 and 15 © javarman-Shutterstock.com; page 16-17 © Matt Cornish-Shutterstock.com; pages 18-19 © kkaplin-Shutterstock.com; page 20 © photosmash- i-stockphoto.com, page 21 © Protasov AN-Shutterstock.com; page 22 © Sandstein https://creativecommons.org/licenses/by/3.0/deed.en; pages 22-23 © © Belizar | Dreamstime.com; pages 24-25 © Mike Veitch-Shutterstock.com; page 26-27 © PD-USGov-Interior-FWS, page 27 © Soulgany101; pages 28-29 © e2dan-Shutterstock.com

Edited by: Keli Sipperley

Cover and Interior design by: Nicola Stratford    www.nicolastratford.com

## Library of Congress PCN Data

Gross Animals / Pete Jenkins
(Gross Me Out!)
 ISBN 978-1-68191-769-6 (hard cover)
 ISBN 978-1-68191-870-9 (soft cover)
 ISBN 978-1-68191-958-4 (e-Book)
Library of Congress Control Number: 2016932729

Rourke Educational Media
Printed in the United States of America, North Mankato, Minnesota

**Also Available as:**